Śrī Mahā Pratyangirā Devī

(Holy Divine Mother in Ferocious Form)

*

Dr. Ramamurthy N.

M.Sc., B.G.L., CAIIB, CCP, DSADP, CISA, PMP, CGBL, Ph.D.

*

*

Title: *Śrī Mahā Pratyangirā Devī*
(Holy Divine Mother in Ferocious Form)

First Edition: November 2016

Author: **Dr. Ramamurthy N**, Chennai.
http://ramamurthy.jaagruti.co.in/

Number of pages: 41

Price: ₹ 75.00

ISBN (13):   978-93-82237-47-1

*****

Table of Contents

*****

Dedication

Seer of *Śrīvidyā Mahāsowbhāgya Parāmbikā Pīţa,* Ayyarmalai, *Śakta* Emperor, HH *Pūjyaśrī Pranavānunda Brahmendra Saraswati Avadhūta Swāmijī,* inspired me to write this book and also gave various mantras mentioned here. He has been my Guru for Śrīvidyā and *Śakta* related areas. I **dedicate** this book in his lotus feet and seek his blessings. His blessings are in plenty available for all the readers of this book also.

Dr. Ramamurthy N

*****

Blessings

In our great religion the *Saṇmata* worship was established by *Śrímad Âdi Śankara Bhagavad Pāda*. Out of these six sub-religions, *Śākta* religion, i.e. worshipping *Śrí Deví*, is one of the best to reach all the benefits.

We worship *Śrí Deví* in different forms. Among these, worshipping the form of *Pratyangirā* is an important one. However, there is no proper direction about *Śrí Pratyangirā Deví* and devotees follow different wrong methods for lack of guidance.

Further by looking at the fierce form of *Śrí Pratyangirā Deví* the worshippers of scared. Dr. **Ramamurthy** has written this book to remove such a fear and to properly guide the method of worship of *Śrí Pratyangirā Deví*.

Earlier he has written lot many *Śākta* related books. This is one more feather on his cap. We pray to Goddess *Śrí Jaganmātā Parāshodaśí Deví* for the welfare of him and his family.

Let all the readers of this book will definitely get *Śrí Deví*'s complete blessings.

ஆனந்தம்　　　　　சுபம்　　　　　மங்களம்

Always at the service of *Śrí Deví*
Jaya Jaya Jagadambā – Śrí Gurudevadattā

Ayyarmalai
November 2016

Śrí Praṇavānunda Saraswati Swāmi
Śrívidyā Parāmbikā Trust

*****

Introduction

गुरुर्ब्रह्मा गुरुर्विष्णुः गुरुर्देवो महेश्वरः | गुरुसाक्षात् परंब्रह्म तस्मै श्री गुरवे नमः ॥

दत्तात्रेय हरे कृष्ण उन्मत्तानन्द दायक |
दिगंबर मुने बाल पिशाच ज्ञान सागर ॥

शान्तं दान्तं तपो निष्टं शान्तानन्द गुरूद्वहम् | भजामि यतीनां श्रेष्टं अवधूतमहर्निशम् ॥

नमस्तुभ्यं प्रणवानन्द अवधूत महामुने |
नित्य मङ्गल दात्रे च शिष्य सन्तोष दायिने ॥

When we talk or hear about *Pratyangirā Devī*, immediately a ferocious form of the *Devī* is imagined in our mind. Also *Pratyangirā* is always related to *Atharva Veda*. Most of have some misapprehension to *Atharva Veda* that it is always related to evil spirits and all. Most of movies add fuel to this fear.

But in reality, it is not so. The forms like *Rudra* of *Śiva* and *Chaṇḍi* of *Pārvati* are also an unruly only. But still we chant *Rudra japam* and *Saptaśatī Pārāyanams* and worship these forms of God/ Goddess. In the same manner, the form of *Pratyangirā Devī* is also abysmal. But the benefits reaped from properly worshipping her are enormous. The benefits more towards removing the fear, evil spirits, evil eyes, etc., - removing the negative thoughts and effects. Once the negatives are removed, there will room for positive to enter.

Various devotees perform *Pratyangirā yagna* using red chilies, which is **not correct**. The *yagnas/ homas* are performed in two paths – *vaidhīka* path and *tāntrīka* path. People following the *tāntrīka* path use red chilies and they create evil spirits. Devotees following the *vaidhīka* path, who really want to be away from evil spirits, should use **black pepper** and definitely not red chilies. It may be noted that we have addressed *vaidhīka* path seekers as devotees and *tāntrīka* path seekers as general people. They are not even worthy of addressing as devotees.

This book is primarily aimed at the giving some idea about the purpose of incarnation of Pārvati as *Pratyangirā* and the form *Pratyangirā Devī*. Also some hints of performing the *Pratyangirā homa* in the correct path.

In the *Vāmakeśvara Tantra* text, as a dialogue between Lord Śiva and Goddess *Pārvati*, we read beautiful verses called *Devī Khadgamāla Stotram*. This *stotram* has 1000 letters and hence called as *Sahasrākṣarī mantra*.

In the same lines, in the *Rudrayāmala* text, we have a stotram called *Pratyangirā Khadgamāla stotram*. This has 2000 letters and hence called *Dvisahasrākṣarī mantra*.

Equally there is another important stotram – *Tārā Pratyangirā Kavacam* (armour). This is also from *Rudrayāmala tantra* text and is advised by Lord *Śiva* to Goddess *Pārvati*. One who recites this powerful armour of *Mahāvidyā Tārā Devī*, becomes victorious everywhere and gets every kind of material comfort. He becomes fearless and gets respected everywhere. This *Kavaca* removes the negative energies from within and from outside.

These *Pratyangirā Khadgamāla stotram* and *Pratyangirā Kavaca stotram* alongwith *Pratyangirā Aṣṭotra arcana* are all provided at the end of this book.

Conventions used in this book: The transliterated Samskruta words are written in italics – for instance *Dharma*. When Samskruta words are transliterated in English diacritical marks are used to correctly pronounce the words.

My humble pranāms to *Śrīśrī Praṇavānunda Saraswati Swāmijī* of Ayyarmalai, at whose instance this book was written. And he has given couple of words as blessings and some pleasantries about this edition.

My sincere thanks are due to all those who supported in this noble cause of bring out this book.

Hope the readers would be benefitted by the contents of this book. The readers are requested to send their feedback.

Our humble *Praṇāms* to all our *Gurus*.

Om Tat Sat

Chennai
February 2016   *Dr. Ramamurthy N*

*****

Śrī Pratyangirā Devī

Pratyangirā (प्रत्यङ्गिरा) or sometimes called *Narasimhī*[1] or *Nārasimhikā*, is a Goddess associated with Shakti, the Hindu concept of eternal energy. She is described as a goddess with a lioness's face and a human body. This combination of lion and human forms represents the balance of good and evil.

Śrī Mahā Pratyangirā Devī is a powerful *Devī* who is said to have destroyed *Śarabheśwara*'s arrogance. *Śarabheśwara* is an *ugra avatar* of Lord *Śiva*. She is also known as *Nārasimhikā* (in *Kāli Sahasranāma Stotram*) – "She, who is the Ferocious Half Human Half Lion of Courage". It is said that when *Nārasimhikā* shakes her Lion's Mane, she throws the stars into disarray. She is enveloped as bliss in the letter 'Kṣam'. In the *Rig Veda*, *khila kāndam* a *sūktam* named *Pratyangirā sūktam* is detailed.

Another name of the *Atharva Veda* is *atharvāngirasa*. *Āngirasa Veda* denotes black magic or witchcraft. *Āngirasa kalpa* denotes a manual on witchcraft. *Prati-Āngirasa* denotes counter-witch craft. It could be assumed that the name *Pratyangirā* is derived from this word *Prati-Āngirasa*. She is supposed to frustrate the witchcraft attacks by enemies.

Śrī Pratyangirā Devī is also associated with *Śrī Cakra*. She is considered to be a powerful repellent of the influences generated by witchcraft. In *Śrī Cakra* worship, she protects the devotees against all odds and guides him/ her along the right path.

The most detailed source for worshipping *Pratyangirā* is *Meru Tantra*. *Pratyangirā mantras* are also given in *Mantramahodadhi* and some other texts. *Pratyangirā* is sometimes

---

[1] There is another Goddess as *Narasimhī* – female of Lord *Narasimha*. This Goddess is different form what we are talking about here.

identified with *Bhadrakāli* and *Siddhilakṣmi*. However it is far better to worship *Devī* in one form as *Kāli, Kamalātmikā, Tārā, Tripurasundarī,* etc. *Pratyangirā sādhana* is done mainly to protect one's self from attacks of black magic (*Dhurmantravādam*) and to prosper in life. There are many benefits of this *sādhana*.

It is said that when Lord *Narasimha,* an incarnation of the supreme Lord *Viṣṇu, ugra* or ferocious form of Lord *Nārāyaṇā,* or *Viṣṇu,* did not calm down after the slaying of the demon *Hiranyakasipu* and drinking his blood. Many great sages were praying for his peaceful form. Still Lord *Narasimha* was in a very destructive mode, which made everyone tremble. Lord *Śiva* worshiped the *Tri-Śaktis* (*Pārvati, Mahālakṣmi* and *Saraswati*) and with their combined powers incarnated in the form of a *Śarabha Pakṣi* as Lord *Śarabeśwarar.* Even Lord *Śiva* was asked to appear in his special form as *Śarabeśwara* (a bird like creature who devours lions & elephants and human combination with two wings of *Śakti*) to cool down Lord *Narasimha.* One wing was *Śūlinī* and the other was *Pratyangirā.* This form of *Śiva* is called *Śarabheśwara.* *Śarabheśwara's* efforts or *Śūlinī Devī's* efforts could not control the *Ugra Narasimha.*

However, when *Śarabha* approached Lord *Narasimha,* he became even more ferocious and revealed His special form as *Aṣṭa Muhka Gāṇḍabheruṇḍa Narasimha,* having 8 heads;

1. *Garuḍa* (eagle face, giving health and counteracting poisons)
2. *Varāhadeva* (a boar face, removing black magic)
3. *Hanumān* (monkey face, protecting from evil forces and returning lost objects)
4. *Balukā* (bear face, protecting in darkness and giving opulence)
5. *Hayagrīva* (horse face, giving wisdom and life force)

6. *Vyāgra* (tiger face, giving protection in battle and liberating from all kinds of diseases, evil spirits and demons)

7. *Gāṇḍabheruṇḍa* (two faces of a special bird like phoenix, giving peace of mind) and

8. Lord *Narasimha* himself (lion face, giving liberation and devotional service to the Supreme).

When *Pratyangirā* appeared, the *Śarabha* form of *Śiva* was then torn apart in a hundred pieces. From one of his wings appeared a huge fearful Goddess called *Pratyangirā*. Her form was powerful, 1000 times larger than *Śarabeśwarar*, her head rising above the clouds and her feet well into the underworlds, fearsome with 1000 faces of roaring lions, 2000 protruded blood shot red eyes, 2000 hands with multiple weapons, 1000 blood stained tongues protruding from her wide opened mouth.

It is believed that her creation came with thunder and lightning and as soon as *Narasimha* saw her huge figure, he realised the mission of his incarnation and calmed immediately.

Pratyangirā was released from *Śarabheśwara*'s wing and then she took the female form of *Narasimha* and calmed *Narasimha* down. It is also mentioned that only *Lakṣmī Devī* in her secret *tantric* form as *Śrī Narasimhī* was able to bring Lord *Narasimha* back to His peaceful form, calmly reclining in company with *Lakṣmī Devī* on *Anantaśeṣa*.

Pratyangirā is the lion headed form of the divine mother. It is told that if her *mantra* is used to harm others for material gains and settle enmity it can react and adversely affect the individual performing such rites. Many of the protective forms of deities also have destructive powers, like *Pratyangirā*, *Śūlinī*, *Śiddhakubjikā*, *Raktakāli*, *Aghora*, *Vaṭuka*, *Bhairava*, *Śarabheśwara*, *Narasimha* and *Sudarṣaṇa*. They all have destructive aspects and destructive applications are described in the scriptures.

The *Pratyangirā* aspect of the Divine mother has been a bit of a secret for most of these past ages. Many believed that direct experience with this energy was reserved for saints and sages. Seeing *Pratyangirā* in any form was considered an enormous blessing and an indication that the person is in similar company.

Pratyangirā comes from a deep, deep place within the Divine Mother. As *Pratyangirā* energy manifests, it is often a very swift and sometimes ferocious current. Many of the saints who have seen its energetic expression have described it as half lion and half human. The lion head is that of a male and the body is that of a female, representing the union of *Śiva* and *Śakti*.

Two sages in the ancient times, *Pratyangirā* and *Āngīrasa*, in their deep meditation, discovered this goddess through her *Mūla Mantra* in the eternal waves of the sound current. And though this Mother was nameless at that time, she honoured those sages by giving the blessings to be named after them. She has hence been known as *Śrī Mahā Pratyangirā Devī*. The *bījakṣara* (seed letter) of her *mantra* is *Kṣam* (bliss).

Śrī Mahā Pratyangirā Devī is all powerful and secretly protects devotees and others. She is always by the side of Her devotees. She is within each and every being in all planes of existence and there to be awakened within.

An awareness of *Śrī Mahā Pratyangirā Devī* has been only quietly known, until recently. Although the *siddha* masters and great *maharishis* like *Śrī Dhurvāsa* sage and *Puli Pāṇi Siddhar* have been devotees of this mother.

Another story even refers to *Mātā Pratyangirā* as having destroyed the ego of Lord *Śarabeśwarar*. She is also called *Narasimhī*. In her meditation verses we have often read "*Narasimhī Krupāsindho, Prathyangari*"; *Narasimhī*, because she hosts the face of a lion and body of a beautiful woman.

Similar to *Vārāhi Amman*, many people fear to keep an image of *Pratyangirā* because she is once again thought of as an *Ugra* Deity or *Duṣṭa* goddess. People who think like that are ignorant of her compassion, beauty and glory. Saints do say "She is not an ordinary deity – she is a great delusion".

She is *Śrī Cakra Swarūpiṇi*. '*Kṣam*' is her *Bhīja Mantra*. While talking about *Pratyangirā Devī*, she is often associated with *Bhairavar*. Hence she is called as *Bhairava Patnī* or *Atharvaṇa Bhadra Kāli* (since *Kāli* is considered to be consort of *Bhairava*). She is considered to be the protector of the Universe, the *Nāyaki* of *Atharvaṇa Veda*. In the temple at *Ayyāwādi*, Thanjavur, she is seated in the middle of a graveyard.

The message that is to be understood is that she is not a wicked fairy, but like Lord *Śiva*, she is the *Devī* who gives us *Gjānam* (knowledge), self-realisation. She is not to be mistaken as someone who causes Death or is associated with Death. By living in the graveyard, surrounded by skulls, bones and burning pyres, she is revealing the truth associated with the birth of human being. We would have heard of a *Siddhar* song in Tamil which conveys that anyone born has to die one day... burnt ashes is the Truth of Life.

Worshipping *Pratyangirā Devī* relieves us from all kinds of evils, accidents, enemies, diseases, wrath, curses, obstacles, and black magic. Those who have *Sarpa Doṣa* or often get scary dreams involving Snakes can worship *Pratyangirā Devī* for instant relief. It is believed that *Pratyangirā Devī* relieves all of us from *Rāhu Doṣam* and *Vārāhi Devī* relieves us from *Ketu Doṣams*. Devotees who have experienced her glory have shared stories wherein by just spreading her *kumkum* around the house or at the entrance of the house acts like a barrier and protects the house and family from wicked soul, snakes and other poisonous souls.

The following are *Pratyangirā Devī*'s favorite foods:

1. *Pānakam* (jaggery crushed in pure water, flavoured with cardamom, dried ginger, etc.)
2. Dal jaggery *Pāyasam* (made with Chana Dal, Masoor Dal, Jaggery, Coconut, Pure Milk, etc.)
3. *Vadai* made of Urdu dal
4. Cake made with Till and jiggery
5. Red Banana
6. Pomegranate
7. Dates

The following are *Pratyangirā Devī*'s favourite colors (for dress):

1. Deep Red (preferred by *Śāntha Pratyangirā* and *Ugraha Pratyangirā*)
2. Purple (preferred by *Śāntha Pratyangirā*)
3. Yellow (preferred by *Śāntha Pratyangirā*)
4. Black (preferred by *Ugraha Pratyangirā*)

The following are special days for worshipping for *Pratyangirā Devī*:

1. *Amāvāsya* – New Moon Day
2. *Aṣṭami* – eighth day in the bright or dark lunar fortnight
3. Sunday
4. Tuesday
5. Friday

The following is *Pratyangirā Devī*'s *mūla mantra* and some simple verses.

Readers are strictly warned that these are to be initiated by appropriate teacher and should not chant ourselves;

Mantra chant during *Śrī Mahā Pratyangirā Homa*;

Om Kşam Krişņa Vasase, Simha Vadane, Mahā Vadane, Mahā Bhairavī, Sarva Śatru Karma Vidwamsinī, Paramantra Chetinī, Sarva Bhūta Dhamanī, Sarva Bhūtām Bandha Bandha, Sarva Vignān Sindhi Sindhi, Sarva Vyādhir Nikrindha Nikrindha, Sarva Dhuşţān Pakşa Pakşa, Jwāla Jihwe, Karāla Vakhtre, Karāla Dhamşţre, Pratyangire Hrīm Swāhā ||

The same *homa mantra* in brief;

Om Hrīm Kşam Pakşa Pakşa, Jwāla Jihwe, Karāla Dhamşţre, Pratyangire Kşam Hrīm Hrūm Phaţ Swāhā ||

Verse – 1

Ugram Vīram Mahā Śaktim Jwalantam Sarvatho Mukham Pratyangirā Bhīşaņam Pathram Mrutyum Mrutyum Namāmyaham ||

Verse – 2 – *Śrī Pratyangirā Gāyatrī Mantra*

Om Aparājitāyaica Vidhmahe Śatru Niśūdhinyaicha Dhīmahi Thanno Pratyangirāyai Pracodhayāth ||

If the above verses are found to be difficult, it can just be chanting *"Jaya Pratyangirā, Jaya Jaya Pratyangirā"* as much as possible. *Śrī Mahā Pratyangirā Devī* worship will take away all evil forces and unsolvable problems from one's life.

How many aspects are there to God. Given that God is infinite, there might understandably be many. Religious teachers and spiritual seekers throughout time have tried to convey and relate their inward experience of God's many holy aspects with familiar comparisons. Many encountered the divine energy representing as female and motherly, giving way to descriptions of the Divine Mother. But going deeper still, we find that there are many different aspects to that Divine Mother energy as well. *Śrī Mahā Pratyangirā Devī*, is a deep and powerful aspect of the Divine Mother. She presents as a Goddess with a male lion head and a female body. Her energy is a balance between the masculine and the feminine, *Śiva-Śakti* unison. This energy has been recognised in a few other traditions from ancient Egypt to Tibet. *Pratyangirā Devī* is the embodiment of *Dharma* (righteousness), *Satya* (truth) and impeccable justice. This Mother devours the negative *karmas* and answers prayers swiftly for a *sādhaka* or devotee who holds pure intentions and is walking the path of *Dharma*. She fills up the cup of a person's unwanted or negative energy and transforms that energy, purifying it. Through Her Grace, a faithful devotee becomes a pure refined soul.

Mother *Pratyangirā* teaches us by removing fear and pain from our lives. She shows us that these circumstances of fear or anguish are caused by our attachments to certain aspects of our lives. A refusal to let go, is refusing to release the attachment which causes our pain. If there is pain or

fear in one's life, there is something to be released, and something to be learned. This release is possible through meditative contemplation and Her Grace. Once there is release, there is Void. The experience of this Void for the first time is like a journey home. There has always been this comfort, there has always been this Mother. Throughout the ages, She has been patiently and gracefully waiting to reveal herself, with her heart ready receive us. It is our choice to take hold of her hand; She has been waiting to embrace us.

Mother *Pratyangirā* gives totally and fully – She is an ocean of grace. As already mentioned She is also called *Atharvaṇa Bhadrakāli* - *Bhadra* means auspiciousness. She asks of us only our devotion and in return she gives infinitely, revealing to us our own True Nature.

Wherever there is sincere devotion, Mother *Pratyangirā* will reveal Herself. This is the Mother of *Moksha*, **liberation** - She frees devotees of their *samsāras*, the cycle of life, death and rebirth.

Goddess *Pratyangirā Devī* is said to have originated, by some schools, from *Śiva*'s third eye. The combination of lion and human forms, which symbolises balance between good and evil. *Pratyangirā Devī* is the powerful, ferocious and profound aspect of the divine mother. The *Pratyangirā Devī* is fiercely protective and thus is worshipped to cure various illnesses, sufferings and negative influences.

The *Pratyangirā Devī Pūja*, *Mantra Japa* and *Homa* are very powerful for relief and protection from various negativities such as witch-craft, black magic, diseases and misfortunes.

Mātā Pratyangirā is said to take form only when there is much to be brought into balance. Because of what we are encountering in this current era, it is written in the ancient texts that Her energy will be here to help all creations at this time. The jaws of so many lions make it very powerful for destroying negative karmas and a great help to anyone on a spiritual path. Though such a current can be understandably rough and it's wise to approach with respect and some consideration of what our heart is asking for, it is with that same intensity that *Pratyangirā* radiates her love, so it is best to also be open to deeply receive.

Thus the Mother Goddess, who is *Mahā Śakti* herself, is the most wonderful mother we can ever have.

*****

Form of *Pratyangirā Devī*

Appearance of *Pratyangirā Devī*

There are various forms of *Pratyangirā Devī* portrayed by different texts and also specific to the concerned regions. Typical of Lord Narasimha, *Pratyangirā Devī*, who incarnated to pacify him also has a lion face – usually have many arms and many legs in legends and descriptions. She also appears sometimes blue.

In some images she is shown with a dark complexion, ferocious in aspect, having a lion's face with reddened eyes and riding a lion, entirely nude or wearing black garments, she wears a garland of human skulls; her hair strands on end, and she holds a trident, a serpent in the form of a noose, a hand-drum and a skull in her four hands. She is also associated with *Bhairava* and she has a variant form, namely *Atharvaṇa-Bhadra-Kāli*.

In some schools In her full form, she is mentioned as humongous, with 1008 heads (symbolically representing the 1008-petalled *Sahasrāra Cakra*, the universal *cakra* of cosmic energy) and 2016 hands, riding majestically on a chariot pulled by 4 lions (representing the 4 Vedas), carrying many swords for removing obstacles.

The four lions can be considered to represent - the four *Yugas* (eras); the four stages of one's life - baby, child, adult, elder; the four objectives of human birth - *Dharma, Artha, Kāma, Moksha*;

the four stages of spiritual evolution - *Śriyai, Kriyai, Yogam, Gnānam*; and honoured the four divine presences – *Mātā, Pitā, Guru, Deivam* (Mother, Father, Teacher, God). Beneath this chariot was an eight petal lotus, revealing the path to becoming free from life and birth is the Eight Fold Path.

The jaws of so many lions make it very powerful for destroying negative karmas, and a great blessing for anyone on a spiritual path. However, such a current can be understandably rough, so it's wise to approach with respect and some consideration of what our heart is asking for.

Here are some of the features and appearance details:

- **Lion face**: *Pratyangirā's* lion face usually protects the good from evil.
- **Thousand heads**: Making the evil fearful; Making the good protected.
- **Two thousand hands**: *Pratyangirā* usually has two thousand hands or arms.
- ***Āyudha***: *Āyudha* means weapon in Samskrutam - she has thousands of weapons for destroying the evil.

The below verse explains the form of *Pratyangirā* and also details the weapons held by in her hands.

अक्षमाला, कुण्डिका, पद्म, पानपात्र, बाण, चाप, खड्गचर्म, कुलिश, दण्ड, गदा, शक्ति, चक्र, पाश, त्रिशूल, घण्टा, परशु, शङ्खादि, सहस्रकोट्यायुध धारिणि, शतसहस्रकोटि सिम्हासने, सहस्रवदने, सिम्हवक्ते, ज्वालाजिह्वे, कराळदंष्ट्रे ।

Accordingly *Pratyangirā Devī* has in her hands;

- अक्षमाला – a garland of beads/ *Rudrākṣa,*
- कुण्डिका – a pot
- पद्म – Lotus flower
- पानपात्र – a vessel with water

- बाण – an arrow
- चाप – a bow
- खड्गचर्म – skin of Rhino
- कुलिश – thunderbolt of Indra
- दण्ड – a rod or stick
- गदा – a mace
- शक्ति – *Śakti* veapon
- चक्र – a disk
- पाश – a snake in the form of a noose
- त्रिशूल – a trident
- घण्टा – a bell
- परशु – an axe
- शङ्खादि – a sword and so on

Her appearance is described as - She is wearing thousand crores of weapons (सहस्रकोट्यायुध) as detailed above, having thousand faces (सहस्रवदने), having lion like teeth (सिम्हवक्त्रे), having a flaming tongue (ज्वालाजिह्वे) and with a wide tusk (कराळदंष्ट्रे), she is sitting on a throne with hundred thousand crore lions (शतसहस्रकोटि सिम्हासने).

The numbers hundred, thousand and crore should not be taken in literal sense. It should be construed as many - countless.

*****

Pratyangirā Yantra

It is usual to worship Gods through *mantras*, *tantras* and *yantras*. Worshipping through *mantras* is called *Māntrīka* method. Worshipping through *tantras* is called *Tāntrīka* method. Worshipping through *yantras* is called *Vaidhīka* method. Whichever be the method *mantras* are definitely used to worship. But which is the main one is to be considered.

Mantras, the sound form of deities, are integral to *Sādhanas* (worship). *Mantra* each God/ Goddess will have different number of letters called *chandas*. Similarly each God/ Goddess will have various *mantras* – probably each one for a particular purpose/ satiating a desire.

Tantras (Looms or Weavings) refer to numerous and varied scriptures pertaining to any of several esoteric traditions rooted in philosophy of the religion. The religious culture of the *Tantras* is essentially *Tāntric* material can be shown to have been derived from earlier *Vedic* sources. And although *Tantras* of different religions have many similarities from the outside, they do have some clear distinctions.

Yantras are some mathematical drawings/ patterns used for worship. There are mathematical construction methods explaining the drawing of *yantras*. *Yantras* mean originally the mechanical, mnemonic and musical contraption in the macrocosm. It is a graphic symbol of the contemplative meditation in the tradition, which was intended to be unified with the Gods/ goddesses. *Yantras* area also called as *cakras*. In a human body itself we have seven cakras thought to be an energy point or node in the subtle body viz., *Mūlādhārā, Swādhiṣṭānā, Maṇipūrakā, Anāhatā, Viśuddha, Agjnā* and *Sahasrārā*.

Goddess *Pratyangirā Devī* is the protector against evil forces; she will bless the devotees with pure thoughts and a hassle free life. When negative forces invade the life, *Pratyangirā*

Devī will come to the rescue. Sincere prayers of the devotees to her *Yantra* will mark the dawn of positivity and happiness in the life.

The waves of energy from the *Yantra* will shield the devotees against black magic, evil eye casting and all other negative forces that hamper peace.

Pratyangirā Devī Yantra

Yantras are great cosmic conductors of energy, an antenna of nature, a powerful tool for harmony, prosperity, success, good health, *yoga* and meditation. *Yantras* consist of a series of geometric patterns. The eyes and mind should concentrate at the center of the *yantra* to achieve higher levels of consciousness. *Yantras* are usually made out of copper or silver or gold. Method to worship an *yantra*;

- Place the *Yantra* facing the East or the North in a clean and sacred altar
- Do not let other people touch the *Yantra*.
- Periodically wash the *Yantra* with rose water or milk and keep it clean. Then, rinse it with water and wipe it to dry. The *Yantra's* color may change over a period of time; however this does not dilute the power of the *Yantra*.
- Place rounded dots of sandalwood paste and *kumkum* on the 4 corners and in the center of the *Yantra*.
- Light a ghee lamp and an incense stick in front of the *Yantra*. Fresh or dry fruits can be offered as *prasād*, as well.
- *Chant* the *Mantra* relating to that deity in front of the *Yantra*, preferably after showering. The *mantra* for the concerned deity has to be obtained from an appropriate *guru*.

Destroy all Negativity

This is a powerful *Yantra* for Protection. *Pratyangirā* also 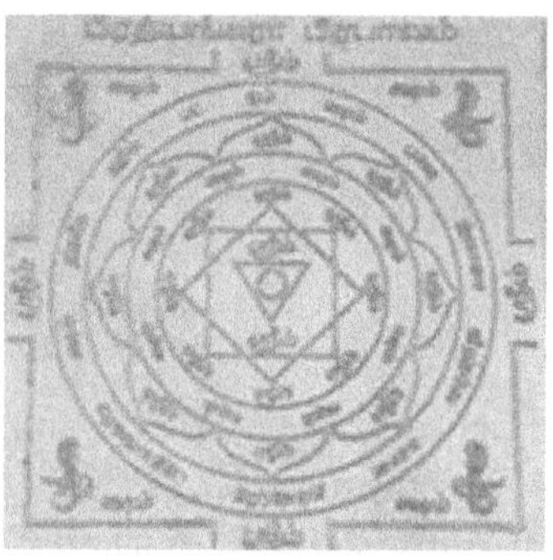 being known as *Nārasimhikā* is enveloped as bliss in the letter *'Kṣam'*. She is considered to be a powerful repellent of the influences generated by witch-craft. *Śrī Pratyangirā Devī* is also associated with *Śrī Cakra*. In *Śrī Cakra* worship, she protects her devotees against all odds and guides them along the right path.

The worship of *Devī* in *Śrī Cakra* is regarded as the highest form of the *Devī* worship. Thoush one or other *cakra* is associated with each of the Gods, *Śrī Cakra* is considered to be the greatest among all and hence it is called as *'Cakra Rājā'* (king of *cakras*).

Thus from every text we understand that *Śrī Pratyangirā Devī* is none other than *Śrī Lalitā* or *Śrī Pārvati* or *Śrī Durgā*. The names and forms may vary. But the mother goddess is one and the same. This is also evidenced by the names in the *Aṣṭotra nāmāvali* given at the end of this book. Most of the names are common with other *Aṣṭotra nāmāvalis* of other forms of *Śrī Devī*.

*****

Pratyangirā Homa

Homa (also known as *homam* or *havan* - हवन) is a *Samskruta* word which refers to any ritual in which making offerings into a consecrated fire is the primary action. Its practice by *'Rishis'* in ancient time refers close to the *Vedic* era. Homas are an important religious practice in Hinduism where they are part of most *sanskar* ceremonies. At present, the words *homa/ homam* and havan are interchangeable with the words *Yajna* and *Agnihotra*.

Homas are an important religious practice in Hinduism where they are part of most *Samskār* ceremonies. They are also prevalent in current-day Buddhism (particularly the Tibetan and Japanese Vajrayana traditions) and Jainism.

Very high level process for performing a *homa*;

A pot filled with water is fixed and the concerned God/ Goddess alongwith God *Varuṇa* (in-charge of water) is invoked and complete *pūja* performed. Similarly holy fire is established and the same God/ Goddess is invoked and complete *pūja* again performed. Then *homa* is performed with the *mūla mantra*. Ten times (*daśāmśa*) the number of times *mūla mantra homa* is performed, the same mantra has to be chant before performing *homa*.

Pratyangirā Homa is performed on *Amavāsya* (new Moon day) and/ or *Pournami* (full Moon day). The *Homam* is to be performed with **black pepper** alongwith other *pūja*

materials. Most of the devotees perform it with Dried Red Chilies, which is a kind of blunder. Only black pepper is to be used instead of Red Chilies. *Śrī Pratyangirā Devī* Homam is performed for destruction of any negative forces like disease, misfortune, obstacles, rivalry and regaining of power.

Goddess *Pratyangirā Devī* is worshipped for curing all illness

and to prevent major accidents and any health issues caused due to poisoning. It is also believed worshipping this Goddess helps in the removal of all mental blocks.

It is believed that performing *pūja* to *Pratyangirā Devī*, pain, disease financial problems will be solved and enemy[2] can be succumbed. One can get the most wanted sixteen wealths by worshipping this Goddess. If *Pratyangirā Devī* is worshipped, all the troubles will be warded off. Generally this *Pūja* is performed with lemon, dates, crystal sugar (*kalkandu*), banana, ghee and flowers. It is believed that the lemon which is placed at the feet of *Śrī Pratyangirā Devī*

during the *pūja* will bring prosperity if kept in one's house.

Pratyangirā homa is also mentioned in the epic *Rāmāyaṇa*. *Indrajit* was performing "*Nikumbalā yāga*" (a sacred ritual to worship *Pratyangirā*) while *Rāma* and his soldiers were waging war in Lanka. This *Nikumbalā* Devī is said to be another form of *Pratyangirā*. *Lakṣmaṇa* with the support of *Vibhīṣaṇa* and *Hanumān* came down, stopped this ritual and killed him, because they knew that if Indrajit completed it, he will never die and he cannot be won by anybody in any battle.

*****

---

[2] When it is mentioned as destroying enemies in lot many places, it should not be construed as killing others – there are different enemies inside every human body leading the person in a wrong direction – destroying those enemies is the main objective.

Śrī Mahā Pratyangirā Dvisahasrākṣaree Mahāvidyā Khadgamālā Stotram

श्री महा प्रयङ्‌रा द्विसहस्राक्षरी महाविद्या खड्‌गमाला स्तोत्रम्

सिंहीं सिंहमुखीं सखीं श्री भैरवस्योल्लसत्

शूल स्थूलकपाल पाश डमरु व्यग्रोग्र हस्ताम्बुजाम् ।

दंष्ट्रा कोटिविशङ्कटास्य कुहरामारक्त नेत्रत्रयीं

बालेन्दु दयुतिमौलिकां भगवतीं प्रत्यङ्‌रां भावये ॥ 1

श्यामाभां वेदहस्तां त्रिनयनलसितां सिम्हवक्त्रोर्ध्वकेशीं

शूलं मुण्डञ्ज शूर्पं डमरुभुजयुक्तां कुन्दळामुग्रदंष्ट्राम् ।

रक्तेध्वालौठ जिह्वां ज्वलदनल गायत्री सावित्री युक्तां

ध्यायेत्प्रङ्‌रां तां मरणरिपुविष व्याधि दारिद्रनाशम् ॥ 2

ज्वालाकाराळां प्रळयानाळाभां भूतग्रहोन्मादमदं हरन्तीं

भुशुण्डि खट्वाङ्ग कपालहस्तां, हालाहलं धृष्टिभिः आपिबन्तीम् ।

प्रत्यक्ष कृत्यां विषमाभिचारां, मन्त्राणि यन्त्राणि वा साकिनी सा

कूश्माण्ड घातीं च कटप्रकादीन् बालग्रहादीनपि दाहयन्तीम् ।

काळिकाम्बां तां कलिदोषहन्तीं कल्याणधात्रीं करुणादयार्द्रां

पूर्णस्वरूपां पूर्णानिन्दहंसीं प्रयङ्‌राम्बां शरणं प्रपद्ये ॥ 3

पाशं कपालं डमरुं त्रिशूलं संबिभ्रती चन्द्रकलावतंसा ।

पिङ्गोर्ध्वकेशी सितभीमदम्ष्ट्रा भूयात् विभूत्यै मे मधुरकाळी ॥ 4

अस्य श्री अथर्वण भद्रकाळी महामहाप्रत्यङ्‌रा परमेश्वरी शुद्धशक्ति संबुद्ध्यन्त मालामन्त्रस्य, उपस्थेन्दियाधिष्टायी वरुणादित्य - अङ्‌रा - प्रत्यङ्‌रा - विजयभैरवादि - स्वर्णाकर्षण भैरवात्मक परशिव ऋषिः ॥

अनुष्टुप् छन्दः ॥

महोग्र क्षकार भट्टारक महापीठस्थित महाकालाङ्कनिळ्या श्रीब्राह्मी नारायणी रौद्री उग्रकृत्या महाकृत्यात्मक श्री अथर्वण भद्रकाळी

श्री मधुरकाळी महा महा प्रत्यङ्गिरा शरभेश्वर शरभेश्वरी - परमेश्वरी श्रीमाता देवता ॥

क्षं बीजं ॥ फट् शक्ति: ॥ स्वाहा कीलकं ॥

श्री महा प्रत्यङ्गिरा महाखड्ग सिद्धौ विनियोग: ॥

करन्यास:

क्षं अङ्गुष्ठाभ्यां नम: ॥   क्षीं तर्जनीभ्यां नम: ॥

क्षूं मध्यमाभ्यां नम: ॥   क्षैं अनामिकाभ्यां नम: ॥

क्षौं कनिष्ठिकाभ्यां नम: ॥   क्ष: करतल करपृष्ठाभ्यां नम: ॥

अङ्गन्यास:

क्षं हृदयाय नम: ॥   क्षीं सिरसे स्वाहा ॥

क्षूं शिकायै वषट् ॥   क्षैं कवचाय गम् ॥

क्षौं नेत्रत्रयाय वौषट् ॥   क्ष: अस्ताय फट् ॥

भूर्भुवसुव: इति दिक् बन्ध: ॥

ध्यानम्

ब्रह्मस्वरूपे ब्रह्मेशि ब्रह्मास्त्र खड्गधारिणि ।

ब्राह्मि प्रत्यङ्गिरे देवि अव ब्रह्मद्विषो जहि ॥

आशाम्बरा मुक्तकचा घनच्छविर्धर्येया चर्मासि कराहि भूषणा ।

दंष्ट्रोग्र वक्त्रा ग्रसिताहिता त्वया प्रत्यङ्गिरा शङ्कर तेजसेरिता ॥

पञ्चपूजा

लं पृथ्व्यात्मिकायै गन्धं समर्पयामि ।

हं आकाशात्मिकायै पुष्पै: पूजयामि ।

यं वाय्वात्मिकायै धूपं आग्रापयामि ।

रं वह्रियात्मिकायै दीपं दर्शयामि ।

वं अमृतात्मिकायै अमृतं महानैवेद्यं निवेदयामि ।

सं सर्वात्मिकायै सर्वोपचार पूजाम् समर्पयामि ॥

स्तोत्रम्

ऐं ह्रीं क्लीं, क्ष्मौं क्रीं श्रीं, ळं क्षं हुं फट् ॥

ओं नमो प्रत्यङ्गिरे हृदयदेवि शिरोदेवि शिखादेवि, कवचदेवि नेत्रदेवि अस्त्रदेवि;

काळि कपालिनि कुञ्जे कुरुकुल्ले चिरोधिनि चिप्रचित्ते उग्रे उग्रप्रभे दीप्ते नीले घने बलाके मात्रे मुद्रे मिते महाऽसिंते;

शरभेश्वर-परमेश्वरि, अङ्गिरा प्रतङ्गिरामयि महादेवयम्बे महादेवानन्दमयि त्रिपुरानन्दमयि भैरवानन्दमयि;

ब्रह्मानन्दमयि पूर्णदेवानन्दमयि, चलच्चित्तानन्दमयि, चळचळानन्दमयि कुमारानन्दमयि क्रोधानन्दमयि वरदानन्दमयि स्मरदीपानन्दमयि मायाम्बे मायावत्यम्बे;

विमलानन्दमयि कुशलानन्दमयि श्रीमत्सेनानन्दमयि सुधाकरानन्दमयि प्रह्लादानन्दमयि सनकानन्दमयि वसिष्ठानन्दमयि बोधानन्दमयि मीनानन्दमयि गोरक्षकानन्दमयि भोजदेवानन्दमयि प्रजापत्यानन्दमयि मूलदेवानन्दमयि रन्तिदेवानन्दमयि विघ्नेश्वरानन्दमयि हुताशनानन्दमयि समयानन्दमयि सन्तोषानन्दमयि;

गाणेशि दुर्गे वटुकेश्वरि क्षेत्रपालेम्बे सरस्वति लक्ष्मि शङ्खनिधे पद्मनिधे;

क्षेत्रपालेश्वरि अघोरे शरभेश्वरि महासुदर्शनशक्ते;

ऐन्द्रि आग्रेयि याम्ये निर्ऋत्ये वारुणि वायव्ये कौबेरि ईशानि ब्राह्मि वैष्णवि वास्तुपुरुषमयि;

वज्रिणि शक्तिनि दण्डिनि खड्गिनि पाशिनि अङ्कुशिनि कुन्तिनि शूलिनि पद्मिनि चक्रिणि;

सर्वस्तंभिनि मुद्रशक्ते, भूपुरात्मकत्रैलोक्य सर्वसंमोहनचक्रस्वामिनि;

नीलकण्ठ भैरवशक्ति सहित जयादि प्रथमाष्ट कोटि योगिनी वृन्द मयूखावृते ॥

कौलानन्दमयि परमाचार्यमयि परमगुरुमयि परमेष्ठिगुरुमयि प्रह्लादानन्दनाथमयि सकलानन्दनाथमयि कुमारानन्दनाथमयि दिव्यौघमयि;

वसिष्ठानन्दनाथमयि क्रोधानन्दनाथमयि सुरानन्दनाथमयि सिद्धौघमयि;

ध्यानानन्दनाथमयि बोधानन्दनाथमयि शुकानन्दनाथमयि मानवौघमयि;

सर्वसंमोहिनी मुद्राशक्ते;

त्रिचलयरूप गुरुमण्डलात्मक सृष्टिचक्र स्वामिनि;

विश्वरूपभैरवशक्ति सहित प्रेतासनादि द्वितीयाष्ट कोटि योगिनीवृन्द मयूखावृते; ॥

असिताङ्गभैरवि ब्राह्मि रुरुभैरवि माहेश्वरि चण्डभैरवि कौमारि क्रोधभैरवि वैष्णवि उन्मत्तभैरवि वाराहि कालभैरवि माहेन्द्रि भीषणभैरवि चामुण्डे संहारभैरवि नारसिंहि;

सर्वसंक्षोभिणी मुद्राशक्ते, षोडशदळरूप अष्टभैरवशक्ति सहित अष्टमातृकात्मक सर्वाकर्षण चक्रस्वामिनि;

मेघनाद भैरवशक्ति सहित ऊर्ध्वकेशीत्याद तृतीयाष्ट कोटि योगिनी वृन्द मयूखावृते; ॥

कामरूपपीठ शक्त्यात्मिके मलयगिरि पीठात्मिके कोलगिरि पीठेश्वरि कालान्तक पाठशक्ते चौहारपीठाम्बे जालन्धरपीठरूपिणि ओड्याणपीठस्थिते देवकूटपीठश्री;

सर्वविद्राविणी मुद्राशक्ते;

अष्टदळग्रन्थिस्थानरूप अष्ट शक्तिपीठात्मक अन्तर्बहिर्महाशत्रु संहार चक्रस्वामिनि;

गदाधर भैरवशक्ति सहित राक्षसीत्यादि तुरीयाष्टकोटि योगिनी वृन्द मयूखावृते;

हेतुकभैरवि वेताळभैरवि त्रिपुरान्तकभैरवि अग्निजिह्वभैरवि कालान्तकभैरवि कपालभैरवि एकपादभैरवि भीमरूपभैरवि मलयभैरवि हाटकेश्वरभैरवि;

सर्वजृंभिणी मुद्राशक्ते;

वृत्तमण्डलरूप दशभैरवशक्त्यात्मक सर्वस्थूल भेदन चक्रस्वामिनि;

कुलभैरवशक्ति सहित भैरवीत्यादि पञ्चमाष्टकोटि योगिनी वृन्द मयूखावृते; ॥

सर्वस्तंभिनि सर्वसंमोहिनि सर्वक्षोभिणि सर्वविद्राविणि सर्वजृंभिणि सर्वभ्रामणि सर्वरौद्रिणि सर्वसंहारिणि;

सर्वबीजमुद्रशक्ते;

द्विचतुरस्राष्ट योनिरूपाष्टमुद्रा शक्त्यात्मक सर्वसूक्ष्मोच्चाटन चक्रस्वामिनि;

कुलभैरव शक्ति सहित काळीत्यादि षष्टाष्ट कोटि योगिनी वृन्द मयूखावृते; ॥

हृदयशक्ति वासिनि, शिरश्शक्ति नीलिनि, शिखाशक्ति चक्रिणि, कवचशक्तिखड्गिनि, नेत्रशक्ति पाशाङ्कि, अस्त्रशक्ति कंपिनि;

सर्व संहारिणी मुद्राशक्ते;

षट्कोणरूप षडङ्गशक्त्यात्मक सर्वलयाङ्गचक्रस्वामिनि;

त्रिनेत्रभैरवशक्ति सहित केशिन्यादि सप्तमाष्टकोटि योगिनी वृन्द मयूखावृते; ॥

मधुरकाळि भद्रकाळि नित्यकाळि;

सर्वयोनि मुद्राशक्ते;

महायोनिरूप अष्टोत्तरशतमहाकाळी शक्त्यात्मक सर्वतिरोधान चक्रस्वामिनि;

ईशभैरवशक्ति सहित मुण्डाग्रधारिणीत्यादि अष्टमाष्टकोटि योगिनी वृन्द मयूखावृते; ॥

विजयभैरव महावीरशक्ते स्वर्णाकर्षण भैरवनाथे महाकाल भैरव प्राणनाडि दक्षिणकालि बद्रकालि रुद्रभूकालि गुह्यकालि कामकलाकालि धनकालि सिद्धिकालि चण्डिकालि नवकाव्यादिरूपे, श्रीमच्छ्री प्रत्यङ्गिरे वटुकेश्वरि योगिन्य: क्षेत्रपालमयि गाणेशि;

सुधामयि द्वादशादित्यमयि एकादशरुद्रमयि सर्वभूतमयि;

सर्वत्रिखण्डामुद्राशक्ते;

शूलिनि कपालिनि पाशिनि डमरुकमयि;

भ्राह्मी-प्रत्यङ्गिरे नारायणी-प्रत्यङ्गिरे रौद्री-प्रत्यङ्गिरे उग्रकृत्याप्रत्यङ्गिरे अथर्वण भद्रकाळीप्रत्यङ्गिरे महाकृत्या-प्रत्यङ्गिरे;

अक्षमाला कुण्डिका पद्म पानपात्र बाणचाप खड्गचर्म कुलिश दण्ड गदाशक्ति चक्रपाश त्रिशूल घण्टा परशुशङ्खादि सहस्रकोट्यायुध धारिणि शतसहस्रकोटि सिम्हासने सहस्रवदने सिम्हवक्त्रे ज्वालाजिह्वे कराळदंष्ट्रे;

अजिने अपराजिते सर्वविघ्ननाशिनि सर्वसङ्कट निवारिणि, सर्वार्थ सुमन्त्र सिद्धिप्रदे सर्वदुर्मन्त्र विध्वंसिनि, परमन्त्रोच्चाटिनि परमानुग्रह क्षिप्रप्रसादिनि सर्वानन्दमय परिपूर्ण शुद्धचैतन्य महा महा ज्वलज्ज्वाला महाबिन्दु चक्रस्वामिनि;

महाचतु: षष्टिकोटि भैरवशक्ति सहित महाचतु: षष्टिकोटि योगिनी वृन्द मयूखावृते; ॥

सर्वतन्त्रात्मिके, सर्वयन्त्रात्मिके, सर्वमन्त्रात्मिके, सर्वनादात्मिके, सर्वविद्यात्मिके, सर्वसर्वात्मिके श्रीशारदे;

महामहामाये महामहाकालि महामहामारि महामहाकालरात्रि, महामोहरात्रि, महामहारात्रि, महाकालचक्रमहासाम्राज्ञि, महेश्वरमहाकल्प महाताण्डव महासाक्षिणि, अखिलाण्डकोटि ब्रह्माण्डनायिके महामहाप्रत्यङ्गिरे नमस्ते नमस्ते नमस्ते नम: स्वाहा ॐ फट् हुं क्षं ळं श्रीं क्रीं क्ष्मौं क्लीं हीं ऐं ॥

अङ्गन्यास:

क्षं हृदयाय नमः ॥   क्षीं सिरसे स्वाहा ॥

क्षूं शिकायै वषट् ॥   क्षैं कवचाय ग्म् ॥

क्षौं नेत्रत्रयाय वौषट् ॥   क्षः अस्त्राय फट् ॥

भूर्भुवसुवः इति दिक् विमोगः ॥

ध्यानम्

ब्रह्मस्वरूपे ब्रह्मेशि ब्रह्मास्त्र खड्गधारिणि ।

ब्राह्मि प्रत्यङ्गिरे देवि अव ब्रह्मद्विषो जहि ॥

आशाम्बरा मुक्तकचा घनच्छविर्ध्येया चर्मासि कराहि भूषणा ।

दंष्ट्रोग्र वक्त्रा ग्रसिताहिता त्वया प्रत्यङ्गिरा शङ्कर तेजसेरिता ॥

पञ्चपूजा

लं पृथ्व्यात्मिकायै गन्धं समर्पयामि ।

हं आकाशात्मिकायै पुष्पैः पूजयामि ।

यं वाय्वात्मिकायै धूपं आग्रापयामि ।

रं वह्नियात्मिकायै दीपं दर्शयामि ।

वं अमृतात्मिकायै अमृतं महानैवेद्यं निवेदयामि ।

सं सर्वात्मिकायै सर्वोपचार पूजाम् समर्पयामि ॥

जप समर्पणम्

गुह्यातिगुह्य गोप्त्री त्वं गृहाणास्मत्कृतं जपं ॥ सिद्धिर्भवतु देवेशि त्वत्प्रसादान् मयि स्थिरा ॥ ॐ शान्तिः शान्तिः शान्तिः ॥ हरि ॐ ॥

*****

इति श्री रुद्रयामल तन्त्रे पञ्चाङ्ग खण्डे, दश महाविद्या रहस्य श्रीप्रत्यङ्गिरा पटलोक्त प्रकारेण श्री महा प्रयङ्गिरा द्विसहस्राक्षरी महाविद्या खड्गमाला स्तोत्रम् सम्पूर्णम्

*****

Śrī Atharvaṇa Bhadrakāli Pratyangirā Aṣṭotra Śatanāmāvali:

श्री अथर्वण भद्रकाळी प्रत्यङ्गिरा अष्टोत्तर शतनामावलि:

1.	श्रीं ह्रीं क्लीं ळं क्षं प्रत्यङ्गिरायै नम:
2.	श्रीं ह्रीं क्लीं ळं क्षं ओंकाररूपिण्यै नम:
3.	श्रीं ह्रीं क्लीं ळं क्षं ओंकारप्रियायै नम:
4.	श्रीं ह्रीं क्लीं ळं क्षं विश्वरूपायै नम:
5.	श्रीं ह्रीं क्लीं ळं क्षं विरूपाक्षप्रियायै नम:
6.	श्रीं ह्रीं क्लीं ळं क्षं जटाजूटकारिण्यै नम:
7.	श्रीं ह्रीं क्लीं ळं क्षं कपालमालालङ्कृतायै नम:
8.	श्रीं ह्रीं क्लीं ळं क्षं नागेन्द्रभूषणायै नम:
9.	श्रीं ह्रीं क्लीं ळं क्षं नागयज्ञोपवीतधारिण्यै नम:
10.	श्रीं ह्रीं क्लीं ळं क्षं सकलराक्षसनाशिन्यै नम:
11.	श्रीं ह्रीं क्लीं ळं क्षं श्मशानवासिन्यै नम:
12.	श्रीं ह्रीं क्लीं ळं क्षं कुञ्चितकेशिन्यै नम:
13.	श्रीं ह्रीं क्लीं ळं क्षं कपालखट्टाङ्गधारिण्यै नम:
14.	श्रीं ह्रीं क्लीं ळं क्षं रक्तनेत्रज्वालिन्यै नम:
15.	श्रीं ह्रीं क्लीं ळं क्षं चतुर्भुजायै नम:
16.	श्रीं ह्रीं क्लीं ळं क्षं चन्द्रसहोदर्यै नम:
17.	श्रीं ह्रीं क्लीं ळं क्षं ज्वालाकराळवदनायै नम:
18.	श्रीं ह्रीं क्लीं ळं क्षं भद्रकाळ्यै नम:
19.	श्रीं ह्रीं क्लीं ळं क्षं हेमवत्यै नम:
20.	श्रीं ह्रीं क्लीं ळं क्षं नारयणसमाश्रितायै नम:
21.	श्रीं ह्रीं क्लीं ळं क्षं सिंहमुखायै नम:
22.	श्रीं ह्रीं क्लीं ळं क्षं महिषासुरमर्दिन्यै नम:
23.	श्रीं ह्रीं क्लीं ळं क्षं धूम्रलोचनायै नम:
24.	श्रीं ह्रीं क्लीं ळं क्षं शङ्करप्राणवल्लभायै नम:
25.	श्रीं ह्रीं क्लीं ळं क्षं लक्ष्मीवाणीसेवितायै नम:
26.	श्रीं ह्रीं क्लीं ळं क्षं कृपारूपिण्यै नम:
27.	श्रीं ह्रीं क्लीं ळं क्षं कृष्णाज्ञायै नम:
28.	श्रीं ह्रीं क्लीं ळं क्षं प्रेतवाहनायै नम:
29.	श्रीं ह्रीं क्लीं ळं क्षं प्रेतभोजिन्यै नम:
30.	श्रीं ह्रीं क्लीं ळं क्षं शिवानुग्रहवल्लभायै नम:
31.	श्रीं ह्रीं क्लीं ळं क्षं पञ्चप्रेतासनायै नम:
32.	श्रीं ह्रीं क्लीं ळं क्षं महाकाळ्यै नम:
33.	श्रीं ह्रीं क्लीं ळं क्षं वनवासिन्यै नम:

34.	श्रीं ह्रीं क्लीं ळं क्षं अणिमादिगुणाश्रयायै नमः
35.	श्रीं ह्रीं क्लीं ळं क्षं रक्तप्रियायै नमः
36.	श्रीं ह्रीं क्लीं ळं क्षं शाकमांसप्रियायै नमः
37.	श्रीं ह्रीं क्लीं ळं क्षं नरशिरोमालालंकृतायै नमः
38.	श्रीं ह्रीं क्लीं ळं क्षं अट्टहासिन्यै नमः
39.	श्रीं ह्रीं क्लीं ळं क्षं कराळवदनायै नमः
40.	श्रीं ह्रीं क्लीं ळं क्षं ललज्जिह्वायै नमः
41.	श्रीं ह्रीं क्लीं ळं क्षं ह्रींकार्यै नमः
42.	श्रीं ह्रीं क्लीं ळं क्षं ह्रींविभूत्यै नमः
43.	श्रीं ह्रीं क्लीं ळं क्षं शत्रुनाशिन्यै नमः
44.	श्रीं ह्रीं क्लीं ळं क्षं भूतनाशिन्यै नमः
45.	श्रीं ह्रीं क्लीं ळं क्षं सकलदुरितनाशिन्यै नमः
46.	श्रीं ह्रीं क्लीं ळं क्षं सकलापन्नाशिन्यै नमः
47.	श्रीं ह्रीं क्लीं ळं क्षं अष्टभैरवसेवितायै नमः
48.	श्रीं ह्रीं क्लीं ळं क्षं ब्रह्मविष्णुशिवात्मिकायै नमः
49.	श्रीं ह्रीं क्लीं ळं क्षं भुवनेश्वर्यै नमः
50.	श्रीं ह्रीं क्लीं ळं क्षं डाकिनीपरिसेवितायै नमः
51.	श्रीं ह्रीं क्लीं ळं क्षं रक्तान्नप्रियायै नमः
52.	श्रीं ह्रीं क्लीं ळं क्षं ब्रह्मनिष्ठायै नमः
53.	श्रीं ह्रीं क्लीं ळं क्षं मधुपानप्रियोल्लासिन्यै नमः
54.	श्रीं ह्रीं क्लीं ळं क्षं डमरुकधारिण्यै नमः
55.	श्रीं ह्रीं क्लीं ळं क्षं भक्तिप्रियायै नमः
56.	श्रीं ह्रीं क्लीं ळं क्षं परमन्त्रविदारिण्यै नमः
57.	श्रीं ह्रीं क्लीं ळं क्षं परयन्त्रनाशिन्यै नमः
58.	श्रीं ह्रीं क्लीं ळं क्षं परकृत्यविध्वंसिन्यै नमः
59.	श्रीं ह्रीं क्लीं ळं क्षं महाप्राज्ञायै नमः
60.	श्रीं ह्रीं क्लीं ळं क्षं महाबलायै नमः
61.	श्रीं ह्रीं क्लीं ळं क्षं कुमारकल्पसेवितायै नमः
62.	श्रीं ह्रीं क्लीं ळं क्षं सिंहवाहनायै नमः
63.	श्रीं ह्रीं क्लीं ळं क्षं सिंहगर्जिन्यै नमः
64.	श्रीं ह्रीं क्लीं ळं क्षं पूर्णचन्द्रनिभायै नमः
65.	श्रीं ह्रीं क्लीं ळं क्षं त्रिनेत्रायै नमः
66.	श्रीं ह्रीं क्लीं ळं क्षं भण्डासुरनिषेवितायै नमः
67.	श्रीं ह्रीं क्लीं ळं क्षं प्रसन्नरूपधारिण्यै नमः
68.	श्रीं ह्रीं क्लीं ळं क्षं भुक्तिमुक्तिफलप्रदायै नमः
69.	श्रीं ह्रीं क्लीं ळं क्षं सकलैश्वर्यधारिण्यै नमः
70.	श्रीं ह्रीं क्लीं ळं क्षं नवग्रहरूपिण्यै नमः

71.	श्रीं ह्रीं क्लीं ळं क्षं कामधेनुप्रतर्भयै नम:
72.	श्रीं ह्रीं क्लीं ळं क्षं योगमायानुगन्धराये नम:
73.	श्रीं ह्रीं क्लीं ळं क्षं गुह्याविद्यायै नम:
74.	श्रीं ह्रीं क्लीं ळं क्षं महाविद्यायै नम:
75.	श्रीं ह्रीं क्लीं ळं क्षं सिद्धविद्यायै नम:
76.	श्रीं ह्रीं क्लीं ळं क्षं खड्गमण्डलसुपूज्यायै नम:
77.	श्रीं ह्रीं क्लीं ळं क्षं सालग्रामवासिन्यै नम:
78.	श्रीं ह्रीं क्लीं ळं क्षं योनिरूपिण्यै नम:
79.	श्रीं ह्रीं क्लीं ळं क्षं नवयोनिचक्रात्मिकायै नम:
80.	श्रीं ह्रीं क्लीं ळं क्षं श्रीचक्रसुचारिण्यै नम:
81.	श्रीं ह्रीं क्लीं ळं क्षं राजराजसुपूज्यायै नम:
82.	श्रीं ह्रीं क्लीं ळं क्षं निग्रहानुग्रहायै नम:
83.	श्रीं ह्रीं क्लीं ळं क्षं समानुग्रहकारिण्यै नम:
84.	श्रीं ह्रीं क्लीं ळं क्षं बालेन्दुमौलिसेवितायै नम:
85.	श्रीं ह्रीं क्लीं ळं क्षं गङ्गाधरालिंगितायै नम:
86.	श्रीं ह्रीं क्लीं ळं क्षं वीररूपायै नम:
87.	श्रीं ह्रीं क्लीं ळं क्षं वराभयप्रदायै नम:
88.	श्रीं ह्रीं क्लीं ळं क्षं वासुदेवविशालाक्ष्यै नम:
89.	श्रीं ह्रीं क्लीं ळं क्षं पर्वतस्तनमण्डलायै नम:
90.	श्रीं ह्रीं क्लीं ळं क्षं हिमाद्रिनिवासिन्यै नम:
91.	श्रीं ह्रीं क्लीं ळं क्षं दुर्गारूपायै नम:
92.	श्रीं ह्रीं क्लीं ळं क्षं दुर्गादुर्गर्तिहारिण्यै नम:
93.	श्रीं ह्रीं क्लीं ळं क्षं ईषणात्रयनाशिन्यै नम:
94.	श्रीं ह्रीं क्लीं ळं क्षं महाभीषणायै नम:
95.	श्रीं ह्रीं क्लीं ळं क्षं कैवल्यफलप्रदायै नम:
96.	श्रीं ह्रीं क्लीं ळं क्षं आत्मसंरक्षिण्यै नम:
97.	श्रीं ह्रीं क्लीं ळं क्षं सकलशत्रुविनाशिन्यै नम:
98.	श्रीं ह्रीं क्लीं ळं क्षं सकलारिष्टविनाशिन्यै नम:
99.	श्रीं ह्रीं क्लीं ळं क्षं नागपाशधारिण्यै नम:
100.	श्रीं ह्रीं क्लीं ळं क्षं सकलविघ्ननाशिन्यै नम:
101.	श्रीं ह्रीं क्लीं ळं क्षं परमन्त्रयन्त्रतन्त्राकर्षणायै नम:
102.	श्रीं ह्रीं क्लीं ळं क्षं सर्वदुष्टप्रदुष्टशिरश्छेदिन्यै नम:
103.	श्रीं ह्रीं क्लीं ळं क्षं महामन्त्रयन्त्रतन्त्राक्षिण्यै नम:
104.	श्रीं ह्रीं क्लीं ळं क्षं प्रेतभोजिन्यै नम:
105.	श्रीं ह्रीं क्लीं ळं क्षं नीलकण्ठिण्यै नम:
106.	श्रीं ह्रीं क्लीं ळं क्षं घोररूपिण्यै नम:
107.	श्रीं ह्रीं क्लीं ळं क्षं ह्रींविभूत्यै नम:

108.	श्रीं ह्रीं क्लीं ळं क्षं विजयांबायै नम:
109.	श्रीं ह्रीं क्लीं ळं क्षं धूर्जटिन्यै नम:
110.	श्रीं ह्रीं क्लीं ळं क्षं महाभैरवप्रियायै नम:

श्री ब्राह्मी नारायणी रौद्री उग्रकृत्या महाकृत्या, अथर्वण महा प्रत्यङ्गिरा भद्रकाळी प्रत्यङ्गिरा परमेश्वर्यै नम:

*****

Tārā Pratyangirā Kavacam
तारा प्रत्यङ्झिरा कवचम्

ॐ प्रत्यङ्झिरायै नमः

ईश्वर उवाच-

ॐ ताराया: स्तम्भिनी देवी मोहिनी क्षोभिनी तथा ।
हस्तिनी भ्रामिनी रौद्री संहारण्यापि तारिणी ।
शक्तयोहष्टे क्रमादेता शत्रुपक्षे नियोजित: ।
धारिता साधकेन्द्रेण सर्वशत्रु निवारिणी ।
ॐ स्तम्भिनी स्त्रें स्त्रें मम शत्रुन् स्तम्भय स्तम्भय ।
ॐ क्षोभिनी स्त्रें स्त्रें मम शत्रुन् क्षोभय क्षोभय ।
ॐ मोहिनी स्त्रें स्त्रें मम शत्रुन् मोहय मोहय ।
ॐ जृम्बिनी स्त्रें स्त्रें मम शत्रुन् जृम्भय जृम्भय ।
ॐ भ्रामिनी स्त्रें स्त्रें मम शत्रुन् भ्रामय भ्रामय ।
ॐ रौद्री स्त्रें स्त्रें मम शत्रुन् सन्तापय सन्तापय ।
ॐ संहारिणी स्त्रें स्त्रें मम शत्रुन् संहारय संहारय ।
ॐ तारिणी स्त्रें स्त्रें सर्वपद्द्य: सर्वभूतेभ्य: सर्वत्र रक्ष रक्ष मां
स्वाहा ॥

य इमां धारयेत् विध्यां त्रिसन्ध्यां वापि य: पठेत् ।
स दु:खं दूरतस्त्यक्त्वा ह्यान्याच्छत्रून् न संशय: ।
रणे राजकुले दुर्गे महाभये विपत्तिषु ।
विध्या प्रत्यङ्झिरा ह्येषा सर्व्वतो रक्षयेन्नरं ॥

अनया विद्या रक्षां कृत्वा यस्तु पठेत् सुधी ।
मन्त्राक्षरमपि ध्यायन् चिन्तयेत् नीलसरस्वतीं ।
अचिरे नैव तस्यासन् करस्था सर्व्वसिद्धय: ।
ॐ ह्रीं उग्रतारायै नीलसरस्वत्यै नमः ॥

इमं स्तवं धीयानो नित्यं धारयेन्नर: ।
सर्व्वत: सुखमाप्नोति सर्व्वत्रजयमाप्नुयात् ।
नक्कापि भयमाप्नोति सर्व्वत्रसुखमाप्नुयात् ॥
इति रुद्रयामले श्रीमदुग्रताराया प्रत्यङ्झिरा कवचम् समाप्तम् ॥

*****

Other Books of this Author
http://ramamurthy.jaagruti.co.in/

#	Title	Pages	Publisher	Remarks
		Indology Related		
1.	*Śrī Lalitā*	753	CBH	English translation of

#	Title	Pages	Publisher	Remarks
	Sahasranāmam		Publications	*Śrī Bhāskararāya's Bhāṣyam*
2.	Power of *Śrī Vidyā*	78		
3.	*Samatā*	176		An exposition of Similarities in *Lalitā Sahasranāma* with *Soundaryalaharī, Saptaśatī, Viṣṇu Sahasranāma* and *Śrīmad Bhagavad Gīta*
4.	*Advaita in Shākta*	80		
5.	*Śrī Lalitā Triśatī*	176		300 divine names of the celestial Mother – **English** translation of *Śrī Ādhi Śaṅkara's Bhāṣyam*
6.	Secrets of *Mahāśakti*	88		
7.	*Daśa Mahā Vidyā*	60	HH *Praṇavānunda* Avadūta Saraswati Swamiji, Ayyarmalai.	Ten cosmic forms of the Divine mother
8.	ஸ்ரீவித்யா பேதங்கள்	60		
9.	*Vaidhīka* Wedding	48		
10.	வைதீகத் திருமணம்	60	Self	
11.	ஸ்ரீ லலிதா திரிஶதி	234	HH *Rāmānanda* Saraswati Swamiji, Madurai	Tamil translation of *Śrī Ādi Śaṅkara's* Bhāṣyam
12.	ஸ்ரீகுரு பாதுகா பூஜா விதானம்	44	Bhagavān Śīrdi Sāibaba Trust, Edapalli, Kunoor	
13.	ஸ்ரீவித்யா ஊடாம்னாய மந்திரங்கள்	44		
14.	ஷண்மத மந்திரங்கள்	150	Agni Trust, Anaimalai, Pollachi	
15.	*Ṣaṇmata Mantras* — षण्मत मन्त्रा:	88	Simshuba Chennai	
16.	*Śrīvidya* Variances	60		
17.	வேதங்கள் - நமது பொக்கிஷம்	280	Simshuba Chennai	
18.	ஸ்ரீ தேவீ ஸ்துதிகள்	131		
19.	ஸ்ரீ மஹா ப்ரத்யங்கிரா தேவீ	60		
20.	*Śrī Mahā Pratyangirā Devī*	60		
21.	*Ekatā*	276	ORIGINALS,	

#	Title	Pages	Publisher	Remarks
			Delhi.	
22.	*Vedas* - An Analytical Perspective	260		
Applied Samskrutam Based				
23.	*Paribhāṣā Stora*-s	96	CBH Publications	An exploration of *Lalitā Sahasranāma*
24.	*Śrī Cakra*, An Esoteric Approach	64		Mathematical Construction to draw *Śrī Cakra*
25.	Number System in Samskrutam	126		
26.	*Vedic* Mathematics	160		30 formulae elucidated
27.	Vedic IT	162	ORIGINALS, Delhi.	Information Technology and Samskrutam
IT Based				
28.	Orthogonal Array	178	ORIGINALS, Delhi	A Statistical Tool for Software Testing
Banking Based				
29.	Retail Banking	213	ORIGINALS, Delhi.	
30.	Corporate Banking	232		
31.	Dictionary of Financial Terms	215		

More books are on the unveil. Let *Pratyangirā Devī* shower her fullest blessings on him to share more of his knowledge and experiences.

Om Tat Sat ॐ तत् सत्

*****